spot

WILD CATS

COUGARS

by Alissa Thielges

AMICUS | AMICUS INK

front paws

back legs

Look for these words and pictures as you read.

mouth

fur

What is that big, brown cat?

A cougar!

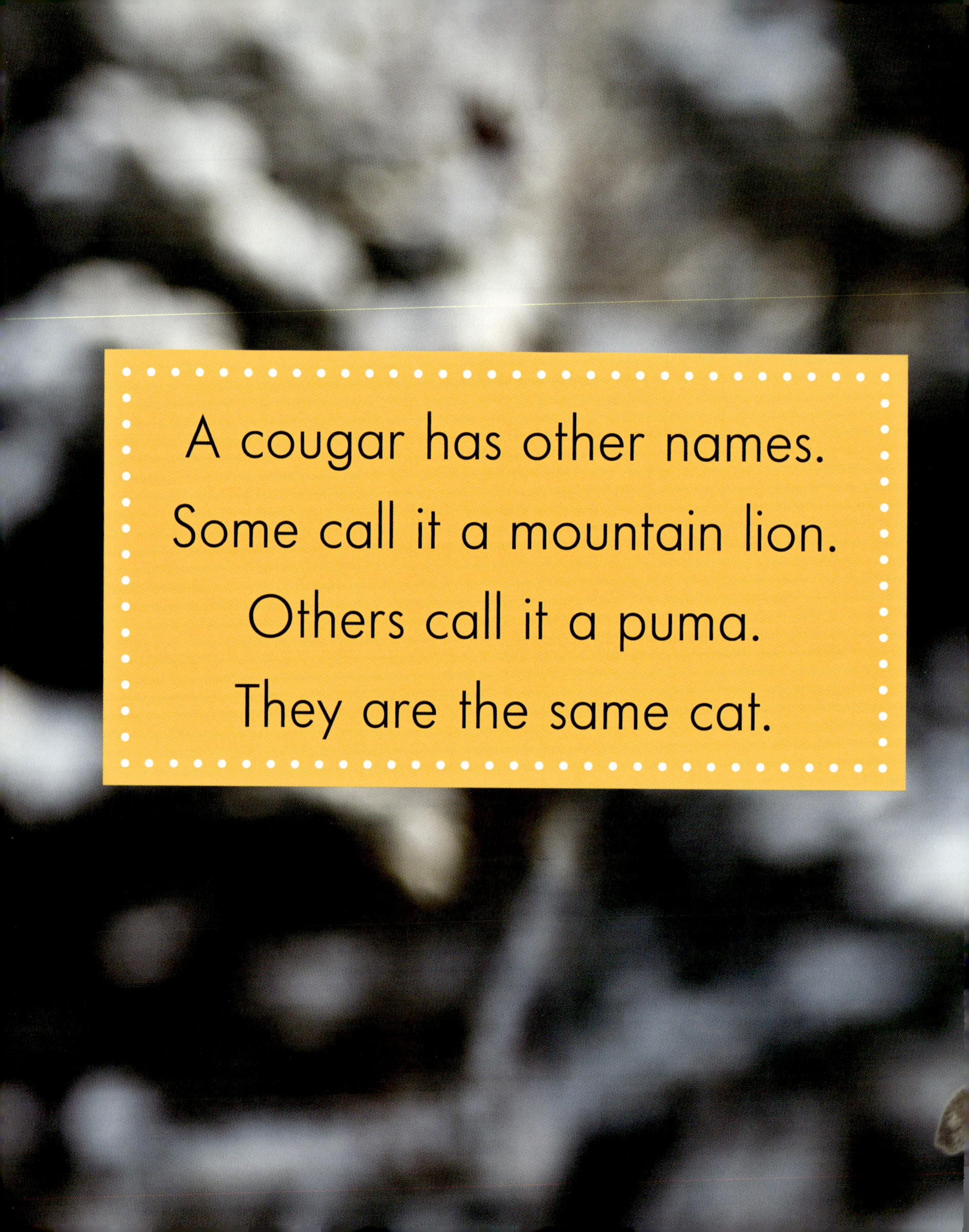

A cougar has other names. Some call it a mountain lion. Others call it a puma. They are the same cat.

See the front paws?
They are big.
They have five claws.

front paws

back legs

See the back legs?
The cat climbs trees and rocks.
It jumps to catch deer.

See the mouth?

Cougars do not roar.

They growl, purr, and chirp.

mouth

fur

See the fur?
It is thick.
Cougars stay warm.

Baby cougars have spots.
They play in the snow.

front paws

back legs

Did you find?

mouth

fur

Spot is published by Amicus and Amicus Ink
P.O. Box 1329, Mankato, MN 56002
www.amicuspublishing.us

Library of Congress Cataloging-in-Publication Data
Names: Thielges, Alissa, 1995- author.
Title: Cougars / by Alissa Thielges.
Description: Mankato, MN : Amicus, [2021] | Series: Spot | Audience: Ages 4-7 | Audience: Grades K-1
Identifiers: LCCN 2019036112 (print) | LCCN 2019036113 (ebook) | ISBN 9781681519289 (library binding) | ISBN 9781681525754 (paperback) | ISBN 9781645490135 (pdf)
Subjects: LCSH: Puma--Juvenile literature.
Classification: LCC QL737.C23 T473534 2021 (print) | LCC QL737.C23 (ebook) | DDC 599.75/24--dc23
LC record available at https://lccn.loc.gov/2019036112
LC ebook record available at https://lccn.loc.gov/2019036113

Printed in the United States of America

HC 10 9 8 7 6 5 4 3 2 1
PB 10 9 8 7 6 5 4 3 2 1

Gillia Olson, editor
Deb Miner, series designer
Ciara Beitlich, book designer & photo researcher

Photos by Minden/Konrad Wothe cover, 16; iStock/GlobalP 1; Shutterstock/Geoffrey Kuchera 3; iStock/Evgeny555 4–5; Getty/Straublund Photography 6–7; Alamy/Vince Burton 8–9; Shutterstock/Ultrashock 10–11; iStock/Evgeny555 12–13; Age Fotostock/Kevin Schafer 14–15